Piano ▸ Vocal ▸ Guitar

# CONTENTS

ISBN 0-7935-9308-5

**Walt Disney Music Company**

DISTRIBUTED BY

**HAL•LEONARD®**
CORPORATION
7777 W. BLUEMOUND RD. P.O. BOX 13819 MILWAUKEE, WI 53213

Visit Hal Leonard Online at
**www.halleonard.com**

# Honor to Us All

Music by MATTHEW WILDER
Lyrics by DAVID ZIPPEL

**Very quickly, in 2**

*Bather:* This is what you give me to work with. Well, hon-ey, I've seen worse. We're going to turn this sow's ear in-to a silk purse. We'll have you washed and dried, primped and pol-ished till you

# Reflection

Music by MATTHEW WILDER
Lyrics by DAVID ZIPPEL

# I'll Make a Man Out of You

Music by MATTHEW WILDER
Lyrics by DAVID ZIPPEL

24

# A Girl Worth Fighting For

Music by MATTHEW WILDER
Lyrics by DAVID ZIPPEL

**Walking March**

*All:* For a long time we've been march-ing off to

bat - tle.     *Yao:* In our thun - d'ring herd we feel a lot like

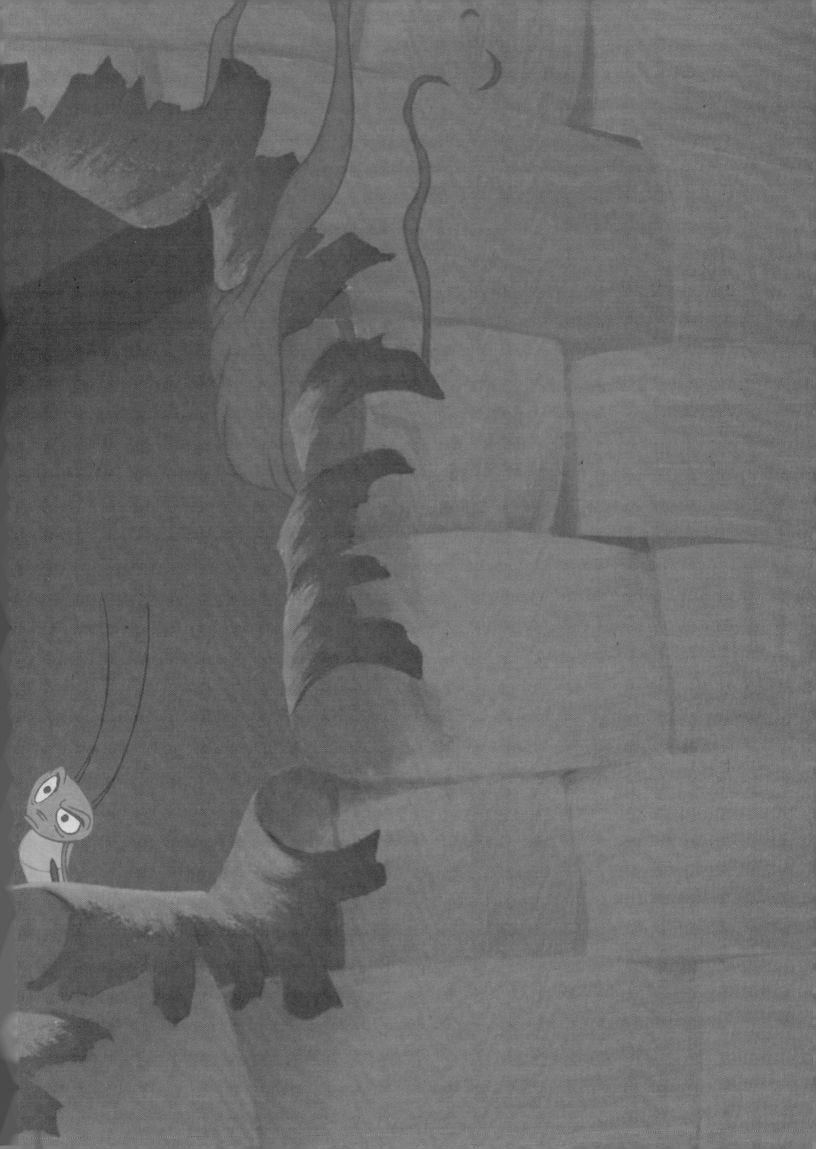

# I'll Make a Man Out of You
## (Reprise)

Music by MATTHEW WILDER
Lyrics by DAVID ZIPPEL

**Steadily**

Be a man! _____ We must be swift as the cours-

-ing riv - er, with all the force of a great _____ ty - phoon, _
*Chorus:* Be a man! *Chorus:* Be a man!

with all the strength of a rag - ing fire, _____ mys - ter - i - ous as _____ the dark _

_____ side of _____ the moon. _____

# True to Your Heart

Music by MATTHEW WILDER
Lyrics by DAVID ZIPPEL

- by, I knew at once _ that you were meant for me. _

Deep _

Ba -

(Got to be true to your heart.)

Girl, my heart is driv-ing me to where you are;

You can take both hands off the wheel and still

to your heart.) __

When things are get - tin' cra - zy
When all the world a - round __ you,

and you don't know where to start, _____ keep on be - liev - in', ba - by;
it __ seems to fall a - part, _____ keep on be - liev - in', ba - by;

just be true __ to your heart.
just be true __ to your heart.

# Reflection
## (Pop Version)

Music by MATTHEW WILDER
Lyrics by DAVID ZIPPEL

**Moderately slow**

Look at me, you may think you see ___ who I ___ ___ real-ly am, ___ but you'll nev-er know me. Ev-'ry day it's as if I play ___ a part. ___